MW00586417

DEATHWISH

DEATHWISH
Ben Fama

Copyright © 2019 Ben Fama

All rights reserved. This book or any portion thereof may not be reproduced or used in any manner without the express written permission of the author except for the use of quotations in a book review.

Printed in Canada
First Edition, First Printing, 2019

ISBN 978-0-9993434-1-8

NEWEST YORK
www.newestyork.co
Newest York Arts Press is a 501(c)3 not-for-profit publisher and arts organization.

Edited by Ashley D'Arcy
Copyedited by Haley Weiss
Designed by Luiza Dale

Also by Ben Fama: *Fantasy*

Acknowledgements

I would like to thank the following publications where these poems have previously appeared: *BOMB, Fanzine, Imperial Matters, Newest York, NY Tyrant, PoetryNow,* and *Prelude.*

Deathwish: for those who kept mine from coming true.

"Those who die old are made of the past."
— Édouard Levé, *Suicide*

Fantasy 2.0

MIRANDA LAMBERT

KIM KARDASHIAN

CAITLYN JENNER

THE HAMPTONS

CELEBRITY BREAKUPS

BEN AFFLECK

BILL COSBY

KENDALL JENNER

JOSH DUGGAR

CARMELO AND LA LA ANTHONY

BILL CLINTON

DIANE SAWYER

MOLLY SIMS

MIRANDA LAMBERT

GENE SIMMONS

JENNIFER ANISTON

JOHN PAULSON

HANNAH BRONFMAN AND BRENDAN FALLIS

JARED FOGLE

BOBBY BROWN

AMANDA BYNES

SCOTT DISICK

JUSTIN BIEBER

CHRIS BROWN

KANYE WEST

KOURTNEY KARDASHIAN

DONALD TRUMP

LAMAR ODOM

JENELLE EVANS

HARRY STYLES

SERENA WILLIAMS

DRAKE

NICKI MINAJ

CELINE DION

KRIS JENNER AND COREY GAMBLE

JENNIFER LOPEZ

SARAH SILVERMAN

ALISON BRIE

JUSTIN BIEBER

CAROLINE WOZNIACKI

NICK GORDON

MARIA SHARAPOVA AND KEVIN JAMES

MARIA MENOUNOS AND CATT SADLER

ROSIE O'DONNELL

CINDY CRAWFORD

KAREN ALEXANDER

HELENA CHRISTENSEN

PETER LINDBERGH

TYGA

NICHOLAS BRENDON

KEVIN BACON

JENNIFER LAWRENCE AND AMY SCHUMER

JERRY SEINFELD

SEAN AVERY

CLINT EASTWOOD

CHESLEY SULLENBERGER

SILVIO BERLUSCONI

BETHENNY FRANKEL

TOBY SHELDON

LADY GAGA

RAFAEL NADAL

KYLIE JENNER

ANDERSON COOPER

RACHEL DOLEZAL

STEPHEN COLBERT

DAVID KOCH

HARRY STYLES

ARIANA ROCKEFELLER

POPE FRANCIS

MELISSA RIVERS

VMAS

KHLOÉ KARDASHIAN

TORI SPELLING

JONATHAN ADLER AND SIMON DOONAN

BRYAN CRANSTON

AVICII

AMANDA PETERSON

CHAD KROEGER

MARISA ACOCELLA MARCHETTO

LENA DUNHAM

ANDY RODDICK

AVRIL LAVIGNE

NORA EPHRON

SANTA D'ORAZIO

ALI FEDOTOWSKY

TOM BRADY

DIANE KRUGER AND ELIZABETH BANKS

JAKE GYLLENHAAL

ALESSANDRA AMBROSIO

MARK RUFFALO

CHARLIE SHEEN

CATE BLANCHETT

ELISABETH HASSELBECK

THE HAMPTONS

US OPEN TENNIS

NICKI MINAJ

CELEBRITY DIVORCES

KYLIE JENNER

AL ROKER

DAMON WAYANS

RITA ORA

JESSICA ALBA

HARVEY WEINSTEIN

ARETHA FRANKLIN

GABRIELLE ANWAR

SHAREEF MALNIK

VICTORIA BECKHAM

SANDRA BULLOCK

BEYONCÉ

THE VIEW

CELEBRITY REAL ESTATE

CANDACE CAMERON BURE

TAYLOR SWIFT

JESSICA SIMPSON

TINA FEY AND AMY POEHLER

KEN GRIFFIN

KALEY CUOCO-SWEETING

LUKE PERRY

JONATHAN ADLER

NEIL YOUNG

BRUNO MASCOLO

CINDY CRAWFORD

SHAUN WHITE

CHARLI XCX

MARC ANTHONY

ALICIA KEYS AND SWIZZ BEATZ

STEPHEN COLBERT

NEW YORK FASHION WEEK

DAVID MUIR

HILARIA BALDWIN

JEREMY SCOTT

JOSH BROLIN

LAUREN CONRAD

JUSTIN TIMBERLAKE

JOAN RIVERS

JOHN SLATTERY

UMA THURMAN

RIHANNA AND TRAVIS SCOTT

IMAN

CHRISTIE BRINKLEY

DAVID BOWIE

NATALIE MASSENET

MARC JACOBS

MARGHERITA MISSONI

GEORGE AND BARBARA BUSH

ANTHONY WEINER

HILLARY CLINTON

RAY KELLY

TOM HARDY

JOAN LUNDEN

CAITLYN JENNER

KATY PERRY

BEVERLY JOHNSON

NICOLE CURTIS

KELLY ROHRBACH

JESSICA ALBA

SARAH JESSICA PARKER

IRELAND BALDWIN

KELLY RIPA

KIM KARDASHIAN AND NORTH WEST

CAMILA ALVES

PETRA NEMCOVA

EMILY RATAJKOWSKI

SIMON COWELL AND LAUREN SILVERMAN

JESSE EISENBERG

CAMILLA BELLE

PINK AND WILLOW SAGE

ROBIN THICKE

HILARIA AND ALEC BALDWIN

JOSH BROLIN AND KATHRYN BOYD

FREIDA PINTO

JAKE GYLLENHAAL

JOHNNY DEPP

DEMI MOORE

DAKOTA JOHNSON

DAVE FRANCO AND ALISON BRIE

JOHN TRAVOLTA

DEMI LOVATO

ERIC JOHNSON AND JESSICA SIMPSON

NATALIE PORTMAN

RIHANNA

Budweiser
toilet
Christmas

swan
ice
star

pushy
Internet
date

unauthorized
card
activity

allow
full
screen

cod
row
smear

politically
off
trend

promises
promises
promises

27

intoxicated
by
melancholy

dreamy
Hudson
Loft

Criterion
ex-girlfriend
Collection

office
space
available

branded
targeted
data-mined

holiday
autonomous
zone

protest
groups
collide

poetry
funeral
party

call
your
dealer

sex
club
relapse

product
in
beta

valley
forehand
volley

long
island
blowjob

repetitive
mass
ideation

wake
up
elegy

dash
cam
attack

wet
coke
summer

cerveza
ad
agency

Queens
horror
subscription

shade
cushioned
overtime

Podcast
One
studio

Mazda
Miata
avenue

better
than
photos

gates
resi-
dential

brave
Portland
Kardashian

caught
on
tape

viral
high school
injustice

rich
lazy
frenemy

millennial
police
violence

institutional
misogynistic
support

tepid
content
strategy

sad
journal
aesthetic

tears
in
Bora Bora

read
somewhere
that

everything's
fine

I
like

hashtag
surfaces

I'm
alive

too
soon

invade
meeting

Ford
Explorer

32

imported
sand

prestige
economy

green
screen

pilot
episode

closed
set

unsealed
pleasure

recalcitrant
hateful

verified
avatar

nude
camisole

give
emotion

affect
bloc

beastly
worshipful

public
shaming

iPhone
ouroboros

Internet
rash

generation
punish

spiritual
menace

Hollywood
beginning

working
death

dead
union

radicalized
suspicion

Page
Six

everyone's
there

spring break

IED

Scorpio

After a Party

       After we smoked angel dust you asked how I was feeling.
I wanted to say, but couldn't, thinking through a deathwish,
tangled up with you, someone who didn't interest me should have been drowning
       in the soaking tub, but wasn't and kept talking as you tapped
       ashes out of the louvered penthouse windows. There were roman
shades in the large solarium, moans from the MMF happening nearby,
          heavy liquidity, strange and lonely, was that you
whose face
       I stroked the cheek of, leather and champagne,
       my wanting like
          a mist spread over this room of strangers,
       satanic courtship dating
how lovely love only finds its truth in death
          dust burning into the plastic daybreak, a plain morning
you wish to sleep alone
       but send me selfies from bed, I like it cruel like this
how the sun rises just like yesterday.

Picking Up Your Spilled Pills off the Floor Is Briefly Humbling

I was humbled when my boss mocked me
for calling from vacation
I'm broke again
until Friday
from my bed
I see the lights, I see
the party lights
it's torture
a post-Fordist allegory?
I appropriated a corporate apology
and saved it
in case something happened
but my end date came
and my vacation days paid out
I bought pills
from the intern I'd hired
before I left
by the seaport
I texted you
we made plans to drink
I like your poochie print workout clothes
the credit card you keep for emergencies
I bought a book
from Strand Annex
whose poetics
weren't to my taste
later the author died
I was nervous
in those days
always in need
my dark heart, my secret
poetry, my baby laxative
cut into my life and love
that it and I may last

1inamilli0nangel

There's a picture on my phone
I grabbed from your feed
it's like a repurposed masterpiece
on loan from The Frick
a one-in-a-million angel
with a hand on her cheek
making me feel like
a down-market ingénue
living beyond their means
in the Kardashian zeitgeist
show me how to feel
when the crystal chips
when my nose bleeds at work
when I can't get in
with each new act of war
another community suppressed
every time I swipe my card
every time I close my eyes

Conversion

Dying is as natural as living, and probably reflected on more.
Thinking is almost always a kind of prayer.

Forever Came Today

Poetry died just before summer
a phone charger fell in the middle of the room
I prayed to neon gods
so hard to sèe a good thing pass
touched by the snow, she gave me a discount
these apps
hates the rich
hydrangeas are her favorite
VFILES in the Hamptons
Lyme disease then a few months of pills
aged into normatively
a subtle thing to say
spent on fantasy
the skaters vaping to Lil B
on the Venice boardwalk
I took a moment
hot pink
disorganized
then floated in the pool
the weather is your boyfriend
I want to buy you something
supernatural sky
we argue
you storm off
I push my hands through my hair
rain soaks a metallic bronze Volvo
it is part of the set
the producers check the gate
the actors can leave
I was into ideas
the thinking
poetry better left
summer's over
this is genius what you're doing here
and your performance at the party
moving so effortlessly among striations of wealth
your performance at the protest

Sun Bath

So evil is normal
and my debt is a pet
a suit to pass out in
and every issue
is a class issue
with a communication issue
transubstantiated
on a summer afternoon
into endless cans of cold beer
and a pill
whatever's around
benfama@gmail.com
a man in definite charge
of his own work
writing a television pilot
like, who isn't doing that
Scientology
Dale Carnegie
debt was the blackmail
the cost that bought the future
now is a good time
to check in with your boss
I quit writing poems
enjoyed tranced hours
as a blue-chip brand ally
sex positive online + glamour obsessed
sitting in the drive-thru line
I looked through all your pictures
you have a gray cat
you don't want to hang out

The Function of Fantasy in the Lacanian Real

I finally get my scene with death on the red carpet at an award show.
An actor who has played me in a feature-length film based on my memoir
appears alongside me before the camera. Death interviews me about
my apparel, asks who I'm wearing, who I'm looking forward to seeing
tonight. Not having had voice lessons or PR coaching, my answers
fall flat. The younger, skinnier actor follows up on my comments with
gracious sentiment.

June Emotional Poem

after L.C.

Even in summer
I miss summer
emerging markets
sieve of massacres
suffering together
at the desert's edge
when I die bury me in
my matching pajama set
with a bottle of champagne
then have a drink for me
it's been so long
tan in Savannah
denuded at Myrtle Beach
feeling alive on a rental car ride
good credit is a man's best friend
deterritorialized production
I'd like to sharpen my tone
brighten the contrast
so nodes of contact distend
to various cultural accounts
dreams have never clarified
anything I've ever wanted
I know there's an answer
if you're going to San Francisco
this sounds like
a poor man's Ben Fama poem
but I am a poor man

Brat Lullaby

So many people I could call
but I'm tired
I'm sick of them all

Work of Art

To be human is to fuck up
having taken speed
I panicked in MoMA beside a Serra
the world, so old
to continue loving someone that has died
Grandma did last night
now I'm going to Ikea
I need to look online
to see if the chairs I want
are in stock
some people can't do poly
this Bay Area guy
psyching out my brilliant friend
a Russian supermodel
suicides in summer
she walked for _____
which looked like _____
my writing is superficial
but pays a lot
the *Twilight* franchise
it's middle-class idealism
and bourgeois aspiration
let's all get together
obstruct our various drives
that seem so clear
when each is alone
sunsets make me sad to die
love forever changes

Ascension Allegory

Friends drive me to Sonoma County to buy wine futures and sample them in excess. A bachelorette party of five, cheerfully, silently talking as though muted, is the only other patronage. I step out to the balcony against the wrought-iron rail bordering the patio. I take a photo on my phone of the lush, generous climate. I am with friends. We hear Paul Walker has died. The breeze carries sweet, hot air down from the far off mountains, through the grapevines, to where I am standing.

I'm upstate New York—Hudson. It's a bright morning, dew glints over the meadows, the warmth of the sun. Everyone I care for is here, gathering around a picnic table, covered immoderately with small vases of flowers— miniature carnations, milk thistle, baby's breath. Containers of hot coffee, bagels, and tubs of cream cheese are circulating. I skip eating because I amon a diet and instead walk the grounds.

Clicked All Your Links

I just said I didn't know
and now you are saying
you aren't sure I'm cool
that's cool
I was thinking
before I saw you
the beauty of ideology
if it's working you
think you're above it
the suspension
is exquisite? I dunno
words are beautiful I guess
I like roses dyed with black ink
today I clicked all your links
desultory animated ghosts
that selfie in your search results,
how your website purrs
ugh I wouldn't deny that
haters make you famous
you're like yeah I've heard
so much bad shit, um, you've never
been to Southern California
goddamn there is
coral below the surface
Barbara Guest says and
There is sand, and berries
Like pomegranates grow.
This wide net, I am treading water
Near it, bubbles are rising and salt
Drying on my lashes, yet I am no nearer
Air than water. I am closer to you
Than land and I am in a stranger ocean
Than I wished.

My New Book Is Dedicated to You

Calm, prosaic
slightly desperate
I don't know
I'm an okay time
melting cheese
at the dinner party
it's frozen outside almost snowing
we're getting high
I'm thinking about Colette
who wrote *Gigi*
about a young Parisian girl
caught between romance
and economic exigencies
her name was Gabriella too
were you named for her?
looking at your posts
you're reading poetry to friends
I text you *ça va?*
you write back
much later
je suis triste

Matinée

At the end of the film she turned to me
tears on her cheeks
and said quietly *I hate cops*
I said *oh*
let's take a walk
and if I go to Paris with you
we'll drive out of the city
I'll draw you a bath
in the hills above Cannes

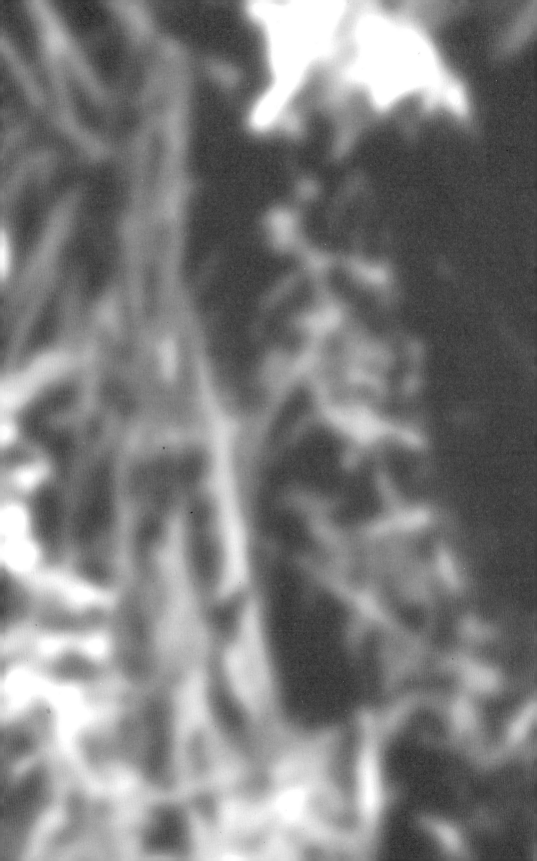

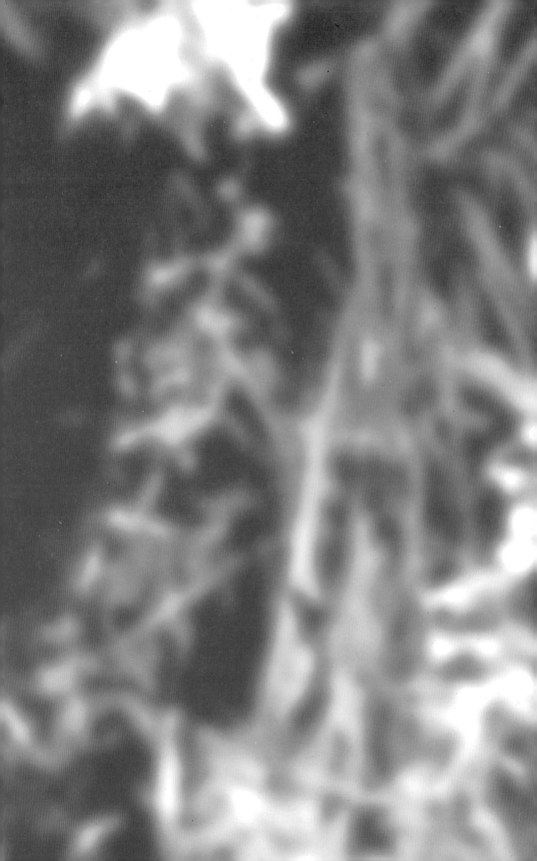

Deathwish

I don't want to die old
too old to die young
inadequate to describe the beauty
of Venice's skaters
I wish for your company
blondes blow me kisses
sun-streaked psycho surfer
the Hitachi is brutal
everyone agreed
just to care
for someone's pleasure

Dommy

I am your sub
and you are my dom
you ask if I've been good
but sometimes I lie
sometimes you read
our sexts at dinner
among the many couples
and touch yourself
and touch my lips
once at an restaurant
you took it further
(I can't keep a secret)
you ran wet fingers
on the rim of my glass

Peasant

Prayer is whatever you say on your knees.

God's Plan

When I'm good
I lick your asshole
when I'm bad
you slap my dick
fucking you with
the plug in
is heaven
if I don't beg
you say I can come
at brunch I see
God's plan
reflected in your
Gucci sunglasses

Loving BDSM

Should die in this condo
it's like waterboarding
when you grind on my face
21st-century surfaces
want to buy you flowers
with no money
can't buy OAK or
Opening Ceremony
wanna pull your hips
taste it better
pull you under
a mound of shopping bags
see you soon, I hope

Dommy 2

I want to tell you
but can't
what it feels like
when I tug down your panties
and my mouth floods
chaotic urges
it's like Waterford crystal
an experience outside language
your pussy tastes like
Versace nightgowns
Chanel pom-poms
the wand I want to lick
just to touch your skin
and smell your neck
to become your vampire
to kiss and smell you
right now and forever
you say Hitachi hurts you
that breaks my heart
and I want to kiss it
I will always kiss it
kiss it kiss it better baby

My Chemical Romance

Biting your titties
on PCP

Vampire Gloves

When I eat sushi
in the green room toilet
of The Standard hotel
when my bruised cheeks
slink into office chairs
when nudes drain my data
I feel mastery
over the symbolic order
trust no client
daddies wanna fuck
for free, they cry
I only have so
much cash on me
I want to kill, instead
I wash your clothes
in a bath of peppermint
and softening oils
you outline the poly canon
later you mistreat
my goat milk ass

Vampire Gloves 2

I brought her snacks and Pellegrino
she made me memes
I wash her in a bath of peppermint
I want roses all the time, just because

Easy Peasant Dick

You tell me to fave your tweets
but I'm just reading them at work:
i'm autumn all year
life is knowing what it's like
oh no my heart feels bad
everyone needs to get out of my body
I think there's a Samhain roaring inside you, the dark mirror
of the Beltane we'd celebrated watching
television eating biscuits in the bath, hitting
the bowl as I brought you things
there are people our age
blacking out at brunch
avenues lined with ailanthus
I wish to kill
as a peasant might
in the brown blunted rain
it seems beautiful
and a moving experience
I'm a serf
in the bed
you make me soak
in the barrel out back
my body gets no rest
a simple mind
holds complex drives
I doesn't understand
many words you say
when you sit on my face
you say Ashes,
eat your stew
it'll keep your
ass creamy
and make your
easy dick hard
when you suck me
it's like rain
on the wilted fields

when you come
it's the harvest
the reaper
is watching in the woods

Choker

Yeah I eat ass
and if I die
before I wake
I give my domme
my bones to take
to Santa Cruz
above the sea
and make a choker
finally from
my ashes
and wear it
around her sexy
sexy sexy neck

Lonely Peasant

My roof
my life
my loneliness
is killing me
I'm often confused
it's good
to have a crush
on you, I wanted
a fling, I got
scuffed cheeks
overdraft fees
I love how
your eyes close
in daylight
kiss me
if I plead
a begging castrato
to suck your tongue
acting out
for a bruise
pull my hair
text me wet dreams
oh hit me baby
let my bruises
show at work
hit me up
if only just
one more time

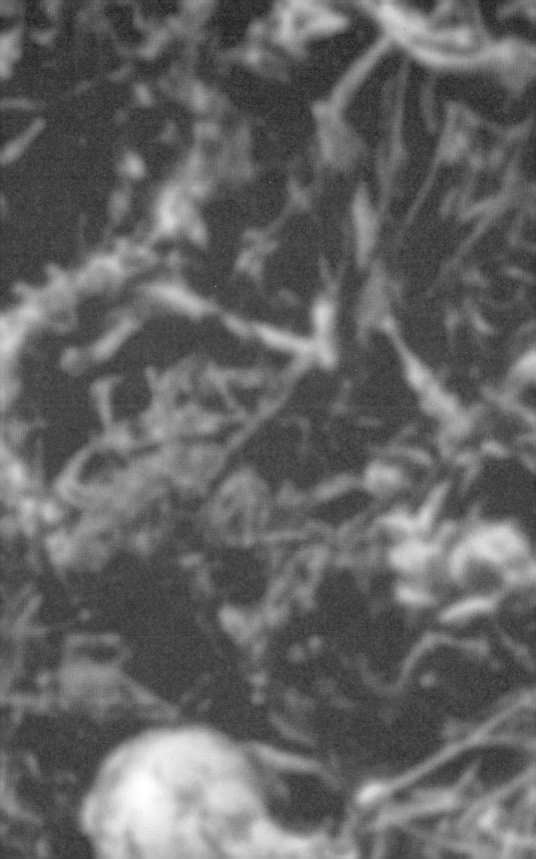

Wet Hair

Yesterday you went to the desert
I put on Brahms channel
and washed the tub
my fur stood up
seeing your picture
in my feed
pool boys change your towels
another violent news cycle
you're partying with a friend
it's very maybe she's born with it

Jennifer they'd have named me
time I can't get back
the Anthropocene is a fucked-up time to be alive
yet mint grows
a chemical peel
a party in bungalow five
you're back one month
I need to chill
with you in the desert
days of war
nights of love
the more things change
things more the

a collage of consciousness
pleasures of an empty mind
wet hair in the basement
S&M waterboarding training
Trisha told us about
Restylane, Juvéderm, Dysport
emerald, blood, ash
with this Apple appliance
I can be a better ally

I felt embarrassed walking the city
like someone in a fiction
I'd sent a photo
of the strawberries
I'd had for breakfast
leftover from a work thing
saw your face
on a billboard
I will probably jump from
let's watch *Mondo Cane*

A bigger splash
God is this actual pool
gloved hands pitter ashes
into the pool
witness the people
fuck you're on molly again
grace to live, to see
"Gymnopédie No. 4" on a grave
that aching deal we'd made
of ourselves

views between the legs of dancers
my mind is a haunted house
flesh I can't touch
I can't save your life meditating
on a tattoo that says brut
the neighbors are banging
to Rihanna, "Kiss It Better"
it's a perfect song, all slow
its strength growing
how I wish if the world ends tomorrow
you would text me today
don't worry about a thing
don't worry baby

You lay there
an entire system breathing
and more
this poem has a riding crop
and a body under
the girlfriend experience in Mykonos
no don't waste that blowout
let's go regard model
boats in the park no
let's all Uber to the beach
for sunset then
stay up drinking
unregarding the nation

I feel cruel optimism
with you it's cool
Gucci streetwear at Maison Premiere
that actual condo in the clouds
just wanna breathe your air
grab your hair
Sunday dusk
you're looking through your phone
for you it's just
another late night out

I'm a client
when you send me videos
you make for clients

There's French theory
in these Uniqlo joggers
amber moves
crystal fairies
life's rich pageant
all your poses on the internet
she texts me
she texts me not

Come over …
wait did you move to LA?
oh
you're in SoHo?
I have to walk a dog in Chelsea wanna come by?
no … that's Sunday
I'm starving, all I've had today was avocado toast
and a bag of Flamin' Hot Cheetos
(sounding resigned) oh okay
I'm sorry I haven't read your book yet
it's on my Kindle for the trip

Everything you see
is an ad for something
you can imagine
that media guy you've been hanging out with
I hope you turn his adulation into money
at least my good mood is holding

Heyyyy it's Ben ... sorry to leave a voicemail, I really hate it when people do that buttttt ...just wanted to see what you were up too this weekend and next week ... we'd talked about getting picklebacks at that place in Williamsburg(?) so I guess just ... let me know?
Okay

Bye

Ashes

The horizon stays there

money proliferates

someone is dying in Miami, near a pool

to endure is to endure among loss or lack

I've never felt exhausted by beauty

but I'm tired of describing it

the sea keeps moving

emotions are only there

romantic and legendary

I remember everything

who's going to zip

your dress up in the morning

I remember square beginnings and endings to summer

hangovers and coke bloat

the first time I was asked for a nude

I remember the first one she sent me

Anton, allergic to summer, my heart, injected shots

on weekends we'd mix coke and Ketamine: cocquettemine

I wanted to shoot it, sweet grasses of June

later, in love, crushing Oxy

I OD'd my friend, he lived, ha ha, oh man

miracle motherfucker, right there at the orgy

Fentanyl hickies

day job bruises

love wearing camo

how it became fashion

can't name five places

this country is occupying

I was looking for the language

of the 21st century

the body persists long after the words

that make it desirable have been used up

I saw my reflection in a pile of trash

sometimes I really don't know what I'm doing